ACKNOWLEDGMENT

Writing a book has always been a dream of mine. Birthing it was not easy, but it is more

rewarding than I could have ever imagined. I am eternally grateful to God for planting the seed
and dream inside of me.
None of this would have been possible without the support of my husband, Adegbola Ajayi.
Thank you for believing in me, supporting me and cheering me on.
I am eternally blessed by my children, Ara and Ore Ajayi. They inspire me daily to be a better person and to stay true to myself.

I wouldn't be here without the unconditional love and support of my parents, Samuel and Tomike James.
Of course, my life and this book wouldn't be what it is without the counsel and voices of the world's greatest sisters, Olayide Ola-Thomas and Modesola Akala.
To my editor, Adeola Fadumiye, thank you for bringing my vision to life
Finally, to my illustrator, Shina Ajulo, thank you for capturing my vision

SUMMARY

This book "Ara" is a story of Ara and her grandma. This reflects the importance of positive affirmation and a change in perspective to see the good in every day.
Ara means wonder, and her grandma is quick to tell her all the wonderful things that she is. She is beautiful. She is brave. She is smart. It is all the things Ara knows she is and wants to be.
But not everyone sees the wonder, beauty, bravery and smarts that her grandma sees and sings over her.
What happens when it rains and it feels like the sun isn't shining?
Ara needed a change in perspective and to see wonder even in places instances that are cloudy.
In this debut children's book, Tolu Ajayi pens a story she is all too familiar with as a Nigerian-American living in America.
Ara, the wonder child, steals our heart as she navigates her world. Her story is heartwarming and beautiful and will inspire you to see the wonder in each day.

My name is Ara.
I am African. My name means wonder.

Every morning, when the sun rises, my grandma wakes me up with a praise poem.

"Ara, wake up to a good day.
Ara, today will be a good day.
Ara, you are great."

While I get ready for school, she continues in her sweet voice.

"Ara,
You are beautiful.
You are smart.
You are brave."

It is our special morning tradition. Sometimes at breakfast, mom and dad join in!

Her praise poem makes me happy.

Before I leave the house for school, Mama hugs me and whispers,

"Your name is Ara,
You are beautiful.
You are smart.
You are brave."

I skip out the door, excited to go to school and say out loud

"My name is Ara.
I am beautiful.
I am smart.
I am brave."

But today at school, Suzie made fun of my skin. She called me "Blackie" and made me sad.

I said to myself, "I am beautiful." Then I said to her "my skin is beautiful," but I still felt sad.

During lunch, David said my food stinks. Everyone laughed.
I said to myself "I am brave."
Even though I was scared, I told him, "Jollof rice is my favorite food, and it is yummy."

After lunch, we got our math quiz back. I got an "A".
I reminded myself "I am smart,"

When I got home from school, I told Mama: "Today was not a great day. The kids at school made fun of my skin and my food, buuuuut I got an "A" on my math quiz.

Grandma says, See Ara, You are smart!
Everyday is not a sunny day. But even on cloudy days, if you look close enough you will find reasons to have a good day."

"Today is still a great day!
Ara,
You are still beautiful.
You are still brave.
You are still smart."

Today, Mama woke me up with a praise poem.

"Ara, wake up to a good day.
Ara, today will be a good day.
Ara, you are great"

Before I head out of the door to school, Mama hugs me and whispers,

"Your name is Ara,
You are beautiful.
You are smart.
You are brave."

In the hall way Suzie made fun of how I dressed.
It made me sad. I remember what Mama said,

"today is still a great day and I am beautiful."

At recess, I fell face down while running and some of the kids laughed. I remember what Mama said,

"today is still a great day and I am brave".

After recess, we played a new game in my class. I did not win the first round. I remember what Mama said,

"today is still a great day and I am smart".

When I got home from school, I couldn't wait to tell Mama about my day.

Today was a great day Mama!
My teacher loved my dress.
I had fun at recess, and
I learned a new game.
Today was a great day!

My name is _____.
I am beautiful/handsome.
I am smart.
I am brave.

Appendix

Ara's name is from the western part of Nigeria in West Africa.
Jollof rice is a west African cuisine, and several countries have variations of jollof rice.
Mama is what some parts of Nigeria call their grandma.
Praise poem/poetry: This is indigenous to the Yoruba tribe of West Africa. The Yoruba word for praise poem/ poetry is Oriki.

AutoBiography

Tolulope Ajayi is a Nigerian-American book author. She is passionate about keeping her culture alive by telling the stories of the everyday lives and experiences of African children. She translates this dedication into writing children's books.
She earned her Bachelor of Science in Health Science from Howard University and a Doctor of Physical Therapy degree from Neumann University. She has been practicing for seven years.

When she isn't treating her patients, you can find her dreaming up a new story to write, travelling and reading. Born and raised in Lagos, Nigeria, she now lives in Austin, Texas with her husband and two (2) children. This is her first book and it is inspired by her relationship with her grandma.

All rights reserved No part of this book may be reproitted in any form or by any means, electronic, mechanical, photocopying, recording, or otherwise, without express written permission of the publisher.

Printed in the United States of America

Lightning Source UK Ltd.
Milton Keynes UK
UKHW050257140921
390506UK00002B/148